NOBODY'S PERF

NOBODY'S PERFECT

REFUGEES WRITING IN WALES

2

edited by

Eric Ngalle Charles

Tom Cheesman

and

Sylvie Hoffmann

Swansea
Hafan Books
2004

ISBN 0–9545147–1–8

Cover art-work by Farahnaz Mortazavi.

Frontispiece courtesy of Shahid Altaf.

Maxson Sahr Kpakio acknowledges the use of texts by Richard Carlson and Christopher Cox in his "Progress and True Progress".

Published by Hafan Books   First impression 2004

Hafan Books is a non-profit publisher associated with Swansea Bay Asylum Seekers Support Group. SBASSG is a community group run by asylum seekers, refugees and other local people.

Hafan Books and **SBASSG** c/o
The Heyokah Centre
2 Humphrey Street
Swansea
SA1 6BG

Website: **www.hafan.org**   E-mail: **hafanbooks@yahoo.co.uk**

All proceeds from sales of this book are used to support asylum seekers and refugees through SBASSG and the Welsh Refugee Council, and especially to assist those left destitute and homeless by the National Asylum Support Service.

The editors thank the contributors, the translators and the encouragers, who all gave their work free of charge. Printing costs were offset by the advertisers and by several individual, anonymous donors, whom we warmly thank.

Designed by Tom Cheesman.   Printed in Wales by Gwasg Gomer.

Contents

For Lauraann Grobler

Gwyn ei byd yr oes a'u clyw,
Dangnefeddwyr, plant i Dduw.

Introduction

Tom Cheesman

Nobody's Perfect was conceived and created in about two months, just like *Between a Mountain and a Sea* last year. We the editors can do this because we know a lot of asylum seekers and refugees through our volunteer work and/or paid work. We've decided now that we'll do it every year.

Why do we do it? Because asylum seekers (meaning people waiting to hear whether they're allowed to stay here) and refugees (meaning people who've been allowed to stay here, if only conditionally and temporarily) have too few opportunities to make themselves heard. Because too many British people believe the simple, demonising myths and the poisonous confusions peddled by many journalists and politicians. Because the process of writing can be therapeutic, and to be asked to write – or helped to write – and to be published and be read is to feel one's dignity affirmed. Because there are some damn good writers (as well as artists and musicians and all kinds of professionals) among the asylum seekers and refugees in Wales, well worth reading in any context. And finally, because of the positive feedback since we published *Between a Mountain and a Sea*. The whole edition has sold out – so it was either reprint, or make a new book.

Since the policy of 'dispersal' came into effect in late 2001, a few thousand asylum seekers have been sent to live in Wales by the Home Office agency NASS (National Asylum Support Service – notoriously the least efficient branch of the British civil service). The 'dispersees' come from scores of different countries – people from 52 countries have been sent to Swansea alone. This book does not pretend to represent them all. Each writer represents himself or herself, not some supposed 'community'. The range of ages and genders and geographical and linguistic backgrounds reflects our personal networks and those of the groups we work with – Sylvie and Tom with Swansea Bay Asylum Seekers Support Group, and Eric with Les Artistes Sans Frontières in Cardiff.

Two writers are already published in their own languages, and appear in English for the first time with us: Abdalla Bashir-Khairi from Sudan, a respected writer in Arabic who also contributed a story to *Between a Mountain and a Sea*; and Soleïman Adel Guémar from Algeria, a prolific and many-faceted poet, story-writer and journalist. His work (in French) will be the subject of a translation competition to be announced in autumn 2004. See www.hafan.org for details.

We would ideally have included more writing by non-refugees, and also more humorous texts about refugee experiences – it's not all doom and gloom, there's a lot of comedy, even if it's often bitter or black (see pages 28–9, 38, 40–41, 42–5 and others). We'll try to do better next time.

We've not arranged the texts by nationality, or religion, or gender or whatever. Instead, we hope the book can be read as a narrative. It begins with the voices of children – asylum seekers side by side with other local children. It progresses through a growing variety of moods, styles and perspectives, ranging from Anahita Alikhani's comical, anthropological view of the vulgar British to the deep despair of "The Wanderer", an Anglo-Saxon poem, or its contemporary counterpiece, "The Grief of War" by Aimé Kongolo. The pieces echo and contrast with one another in (we hope) thought-provoking ways.

Sylvie's "Swansea Collage 2" perhaps needs a special introduction. It consists of poems based on conversations with asylum seekers, including many 'failed asylum seekers' and victims of the notorious Section 55 of the Nationality, Immigration and Asylum Act 2002. This says that someone who makes a claim for asylum too long after they arrived in the UK (in the view of the Home Office's adjudicator) is not entitled to any support from NASS. In common with those whose claims have been through the system, and finally rejected, victims of Section 55 are not entitled to any other form of support, either: no benefits, no housing. Nor are they entitled to work. They are quite simply destitute and homeless. The ensuing misery has been well documented by Oxfam and the Refugee Council (England).[1] Just in Swansea, the Welsh Refugee Council is supporting about two dozen 'failed asylum seekers' and Section 55 cases by doling out up to £10 a week each from a hardship fund. This fund is in the process of being constituted as a separate charitable trust.

Most of the individuals involved – men and women, 18 to 50-something, some with medical conditions and one with a small baby – have been offered a free flight 'home'. But they are afraid to go. They would rather be outcasts here. Some have not had the opportunity to make a case for asylum. Others have, and have not persuaded the courts, but often this is simply because their legal representation is shoddy. Asylum work is difficult, badly paid, and unpopular with solicitors. Moreover, solicitors have the right to drop a case at any point, if they decide that it has less than 50% chance of success. They often do make that decision, typically not long before a hearing. They still get paid. The procedure for reviewing such decisions is complex. The asylum seeker has to find an alternative solicitor, or else must represent himself or herself before the court. Much also hinges on the work of translators and interpreters, who are in short supply and can be incompetent or unethical. The Welsh Refugee Council is not adequately funded or staffed to provide effective legal advice for all the 'dispersees'. So we witness many, many miscarriages of justice.

---

[1] *The Impact of Section 55 on the Inter-Agency Partnership and the Asylum Seekers It Supports* (Feb 2004) – www.refugeecouncil.org /infocentre

On the bright side, justice is done in many cases, too. Swansea's most famous asylum seeker this last year was a senior civil servant in the regime of President Najibullah of Afghanistan. When the Mujahideen took over Kabul, he was imprisoned and tortured. Set free, he went into exile in Pakistan. But there too he and his family were hounded by political militants. Following the American-led defeat of the Taliban, he tried to return to Afghanistan, but found that he was still not safe there. So he arranged travel to a safe country for himself and his family. This is part of an account he wrote for us, "A Dangerous Journey":

> I paid him a considerable amount of money. The agent said before the journey began: "During the journey, you must not speak to anyone. You must not ask me when we will arrive. When we stay at a house, do not try to speak with the owner. It may be that you will eat nothing for twenty-four hours or more. You must not complain." Then the agent separated us into two groups, putting me and my daughter in one group. We started our journey early one Friday morning. He took us to an unknown place, a village in the mountains. After that we travelled at night. Once we crossed a wide river on foot. It was deep winter. Twice we spent the night in the forest. The last part of the journey was in a lorry. This lasted 45 days. Then we arrived in Dover, and claimed asylum, submitting many documents.

He and his daughter were 'dispersed' to Swansea in January 2004. His asylum claim was swiftly rejected by the Home Office. He went on hunger strike, sewing up his lips in order to maximise the public impact. The local press and television took up the story, his M.P. got involved, and his case was decided – with a positive result – just a couple of weeks ago, about one year after they reached Dover. Success!

We've decided to make this an annual – a *Refugees Writing in Wales Yearbook*. Contributions and suggestions for next year's publication are welcome any time. We are happy to work with other editors too – if you can encourage or help people to write, or interview people who can't write, please get in touch. We'll also publish pictures – though maybe not in colour.

This year's title, *Nobody's Perfect*, means a lot to many victims of intolerance and persecution in other countries, who are also all too often victims of intolerance, indifference and worse, in this country. Victims in *fact*, perhaps, but not always victims in *mind*. Many retain a good sense of humour – a crucial element in the displacement survival kit. "Nobody's perfect" is the final line of the old Hollywood comedy classic *Some Like It Hot*, in which two young men escape from murderous gangsters by disguising themselves as women and joining a touring female jazz band (which includes Marilyn Monroe). A rich old man falls in love with one of them, and right at the end, he's driving him off in his motorboat to board his luxury yacht, and asks him to marry him. (See p. 85.) The young man takes off his wig: "You don't understand – I'm a man!" The old guy just smiles: "Well, nobody's perfect."

This is the catch-phrase of one of the Swansea Bay Group's most tireless volunteers, Shahid Altaf, a refugee from both Pakistan and Saudi Arabia. Can't even make up your mind which country you're fleeing from? Well, nobody's perfect!

Notes on the Contributors

Eric Ngalle Charles grew up in the small village of Buyea, in Cameroon's South West Province. He left the country in 1997, aiming to join relatives in Belgium, but found himself stranded in Russia. After three years he succeeded in obtaining papers to travel to the UK. As an asylum seeker, he edited a newsletter for DPIA and gave workshops on poetry and displacement to schools across South Wales, for a Cardiff University project. He was profiled in HTV's series 'Melting Pot', and his poetry was translated into Welsh at the St David's Eisteddfod, 2002. He is studying for a BSc in Business Information Systems at UWIC, giving writing workshops, and working on two books: a collection of poetry, *Bag of Letters*, and an autobiographical novel, *Way to Britain*. He has a daughter and a stepdaughter, plays football for Avenue Hotspurs, Ely, and is a co-founder of Les Artistes Sans Frontières, a Cardiff-based circle of migrant and other writers and performers.

Tom Cheesman was born in Liverpool and grew up in County Durham. He lived in Germany and France before settling in Swansea in 1990. He lectures in German at Swansea University, specialising in literature and migration, and literary translation. He volunteers with the Swansea Bay Asylum Seekers Support Group (SBASSG), and is a trustee of the charities Displaced People in Action (DPIA) and Croeso.

Sylvie Hoffmann is a freelance artist, storyteller and teacher, and also volunteers with SBASSG. She was born in Thionville, France, in 1947. She emigrated to Britain in 1973. For four years she lived as an 'alien' and had to catch a ferry back across the channel every few months in order to come in again with a new visa. Finally on 6 January 1978 she was granted indefinite leave to remain. She studied French and English in London and took a PGCE in Swansea, where she has since taught languages and creative writing in various schools and colleges and worked in cultural projects, such as with Travellers. She has recently worked on radio features about and with destitute asylum seekers, for Good Morning Wales with Gilbert John, and with Peter Gordon and Amanda Richardson's BBC TV documentary project featuring the Guémar family, "A New Life". Sylvie has two daughters, a BA from Swansea Institute in Architectural Stained Glass, a licence to fly, and a Welsh GCSE.

Mahmood Ahmadifard has a Masters degree in Business and Accountancy from Tehran University. He is living in Wales with his wife and two young children, awaiting a Home Office decision. His poems were translated by Parvin Leloi.

Yosef Ali, Noser Sultani and **Ahmed Zai** are refugees from Baghdad living in Wales.

Anahita Alikhani studied Art to MA level at the University of Tehran, and worked as a tutor there. In 1998 she began working as a journalist with German, Austrian and Turkish television teams. Detained and tortured after reporting on student protest demonstrations, in 2001 she fled the country. Granted leave to remain in the UK, she won a place on a multimedia journalism course with the BBC. She volunteers for the Welsh Refugee Council and SBASSG and has made a film about asylum seekers – "Anonymous" – for Valley and Vale Community Arts and for the British Council's A Sense of Place project. The full text of "Britain Through My Eyes" – part of which we printed last year – is available on www.hafan.org. Her translator is Parvin Leloi.

Anonymous are around a dozen contributors to Sylvie Hoffmann's "Swansea Collage 2", as well as the author of the elegiac lament "The Wanderer". That poem was written (or perhaps at first orally composed) some time before the year

1072, when a great book containing the text was given to Exeter Cathedral library.

Abdalla A. Bashir-Khairi was born on Dagarty Island in the Nile, near Karma, Sudan. He studied medicine at Juba University, specialising in psychiatry. After practising in Sudan and Qatar he came to the UK as an asylum seeker in 1998. He took an MSc at Cardiff (with a thesis on spirit possession in intercultural psychiatry) and has worked in DPIA's Refugee Doctors Programme and the BE4 project on mental health and social needs among ethnic minorities in Cardiff. His stories have been published in magazines in London and Qatar, where his first collection – *Al-Ruyia* (The Vision) – appeared recently. Last year we published "The Court"; this year, two more stories based on Bashir's experience of the tragic struggle for human rights in Sudan. The texts have been translated from the Arabic by Ibrahim Gafar, philosopher and writer living in London, and edited by Tom Cheesman.

Alice Salomon Bowen is nine. Her mum works at the ARC Community Centre in Blaenymaes, which is used by many refugees and asylum seekers.

Dahir, Dorcas, Olivier and **Susan** are in the same class at St Thomas Primary School, Swansea.

Hamira A. Geedy is from Mahabad in Iranian Kurdistan. She is a qualified GP: she trained in Shiraz and Tehran and practised for 17 years in Tehran and Mahabad. She is now living in Swansea with her two children and husband, having successfully claimed asylum, but she has not yet been able to pass the language exams which would entitle her to work in the National Health Service. She wrote her story in English. It happened to people she knows very well.

Soleïman Adel Guémar was born in Algiers in 1963. He studied electrical engineering at an army-controlled academy, but left after three months in army prison for 'indiscipline' (i.e. wanting to leave). He joined the editorial committee of *Synergie* and then spent two years in Paris, where he worked in publishing. He returned to Algeria in 1991 and worked as a journalist for the weekly *L'Evènement* (banned), then as a freelance, writing for a range of newspapers, magazines and websites. As well as reports and opinion pieces, he also published numerous stories and poems; some of them have won prizes. In 1999 he set up his own publishing company and applied for a licence to produce a magazine of investigative journalism. He received escalating threats, in 2002 his house in Ouled-Fayet (Algiers) was ransacked and his files were stolen, and when he was physically attacked by men with knives, his family insisted that he must leave the country. He suggests that his attackers were working for the "military-financial mafia" which runs Algeria, using Islamist extremists as its puppets. (Algeria is often described as the world's most dangerous country for journalists – 51 have been killed with impunity since 1994, according to the Committee to Protect Journalists.) He applied for asylum at Heathrow in December 2002 and has been living in Wales with his wife and three young children, awaiting a Home Office decision, since autumn 2003. The translations are by Tom Cheesman.

Andy Hyka is nine. He comes from Albania and lives in Newport. We published two mini-stories by him last year.

Aliou Keita ("A.K.") was born late in the rainy season in August 1977 in Masala, Republic of Mali. He grew up in a small farming village of about 200 people where everybody knows each other. He studied sociology and anthropology at the University of Bamako (the capital of Mali) before the events that changed his life and eventually brought him to Swansea.

Aimé Kongolo is from Katanga province in Congo-Kinshasa. He was studying child psychology and pedagogy before he came to the UK in 2002, seeking asylum from civil war and ethnic persecution. His case was rejected by the Home Office in November 2003. Since then he has been homeless and destitute. He would like to be studying medicine. His poems were translated by Sylvie Hoffmann and Tom Cheesman.

Maxson Sahr Kpakio is from Liberia. He worked there as a freelance journalist for two years, and for the Red Cross and the Human Rights Group. Having fled political instability and civil war, he reached the UK and was dispersed to Swansea, where he now lives. His short drama "It Could Happen To You Too" has twice been performed by members of Swansea Bay Asylum Seekers Support Group. He has worked as a volunteer for BTCV and trained as a community worker with the Swansea Council for Voluntary Service. He is a member of the Wales Refugee Media Forum's Refugee Link Group.

Michael Mokako lives in Wales with his mother and sisters. They are seeking asylum from Congo-Kinshasa. He knew no English two years ago and is now a strong writer, as well as a passionate basketball player.

Ursula Presgrave is twelve years old and goes to school in Swansea. Her family is from Pakistan. When her parents claimed asylum, the family had to move several times – from Manchester to Croydon, then within Croydon, and then to Swansea. Now their asylum claim has been successful and they are happy to be settling in Swansea.

Negar Ragaby is 11 years old and goes to school in Newport. She fled Iran together with her mother.

Steve Short was born in 1947 in Manchester but grew up in Malaya and Hong Kong. He moved to Swansea in 1971. He became disabled in 1979 and has since been unable to work. He has had three volumes published, two of his own poems (*Malaya*, 1994, and *Homo Sylvestris*, 1997), and one of translations (*The Gododdin*, 1994). He is divorced with two children and two grandchildren.

Pastor Gabriel Lenge Vingu (who wrote "Bishopston Valley" for us last year) had his NASS support terminated in March 2004. He has moved to London where he is being supported by friends and fellow members of his church. Meanwhile he has submitted a fresh application for asylum.

Martin J. White is an ecological consultant and chair of the charity Butterfly Conservation. He has had poems published in magazines including *Poetry Wales*. He wrote the poem "Running To" in response to a news programme about child soldiers in central Africa.

Million Gashaw Woldemariam, an aeronautical engineer, was a flight safety inspector for the Ethiopian Civil Aviation Authority. He wrote "Claiming Asylum is World-wide" for us last year. He has been in Swansea waiting for a decision on his asylum claim since March 2002. In March 2004 he was refused, and submitted an application for permission to appeal. He is currently waiting to hear whether that has been successful.

Zhila Irani (pseudonym) has a Masters degree in Chemistry from Tehran University. She is living in Wales with her husband and two young children, awaiting a Home Office decision. Her article was translated by Assad Jalali.

Mandazamba Zukele is a young refugee from Zimbabwe, living in Cardiff.

A Dream

Michael Mokako

*This poem was written soon after Michael and his family
learned that their asylum application had been refused.
They are now waiting to hear whether their appeal has been
successful.*

We dream our worry
Our wish which will be reality soon

May those without hope find welcome here
May those without hope of success be able to succeed

Welcome to the will that will be act soon
Welcome to the hands on the edge of taking me through
Welcome to the community longing to understand

May our seeking be found
May our dreams and hopes find hospitality

Let's Get Along

Alice Salomon Bowen

My name's Alice. I'm only nine but I've learnt to respect other people's cultures. I think people from different countries should get along with each other. Just because they are different doesn't mean they are bad or trying to hurt us in any way. From my experiences, all the people I have met have all been very nice. People treat you like you treat them.

Friendship

Friends of all SHAPES
Friends of all SIZES
Friends of all COLOURS
Friends of all NATIONS
Friends of all CULTURES
Friends of TODAY
Friends of TOMORROW
Friends FOREVER

Imagine

Imagine if war broke out here

You would want to move

Maybe to another country but just

Imagine they kicked you out and sent you back here

How would you feel?

Just think about that.

Sunday 11 March 2001

Andy Hyka

On that day in Macedonia the police were knocking everybody's door because said a lie at the police the police saying to everybody who was saying a lie and somebody told a lie and they said like it was us they he said search the house but it wasn't us it was somebody else so the police came and knocked and knocked our door and I ran into the house because I was playing in the front door with my Grompa but they got my Grompa and hit him and and they hanged him up.

The Dog House

Negar Ragaby

Can we make a house in the garden for the dog? He wants something to sleep in, said Pat.

I will ask Dad if we can have something to make a little house with, said Sam.

Dad was up on the house but Sam just shouted. We can have all this, can you help me? Look, we must work fast. This will be a good little house, said Pat. The dog will like this house. Look at the cat, she wants something now. She can sleep at home with me, says Sam. Look dad, it's a good little house but now we need something to eat. Oh look! Help! Run fast into the house! The dog lay in the little house. He likes it there. Where is the cat? Is she in the garden? No, she came in the house with me. She's here!

I will ask Dad if we can have something for our tea. We'll have to get something from the shops. We'll run up the street to the good shops and get it all in there. Look at the dog. He wants to come with us. Let him come. He can run fast.

Look at all of this. There is something for the dog, something for the cat, and all this for our tea.

Sam and Pat had their tea in the little house.

The Volcano in My Life

Ursula Presgrave

Please read my poem from the bottom line up!

Warm and painful
Lava-tears run down my cheeks
Happens!
What
That is exactly!
Myself!
Within
Explode
It is going to
A bit more
Crack and shake
Up
It starts to move
It starts to shake and crack
A volcano of tears grows inside me

Home or Away?

Dahir, Dorcas, Olivier and Susan

I want to stay here because I like this school.

I want to go home because my friends are there.

I want to stay here because I can see things

I couldn't see in my old life.

I never saw the sea until I came here.

I want to go home because I like the teachers.

I want to stay here because there are buses to take you to

London, Birmingham or Cardiff.

Buses don't go that far at home.

I want to stay here so that in the summer

I will be able to go to the beach.

I want to go home to see my father.

I want to stay here.

I want to go home.

An Ageing Woman

Eric Charles with Mandazamba Zukele

She's seen this little boy
Pace up and down the streets
Every morning

Face down he walks
Back and forth
His hands on his back

One day she asks
Little one, morning and night
I see you walk up and down
Now, who is your father

He replies gently
Mugabe
Shocked she asks
So who is your mother

With a sad look he says
Zimbabwe

And what do you want to be
When you grow up
She asks

Crying he says
An orphan

Running To

Martin White

My son would have been a mechanic
He was clever with engines
But soldiers took him
Gave him food stolen from villages
Showed him how to hold a weapon
To march in line with other boys
To wear a peaked cap
The soldiers laughed
And he thought it was a game
But when they were gone so was my son
He was eleven then

Sometimes when we had no food
My daughter came back from the town
With rice or oil
Told me she stole it
And that was bad enough
I tried not to think
But I heard how men spoke about her
She's bright like her mother
She wasn't yet fourteen

My wife has diplomas
She's a teacher
But no-one round here had money
To send their children to school

She worked in the fields
Leaving before first light
Returning after dark

When I married her
She was tall and straight
Now she's burdened
By my blindness
They say it could be cured
For a few American dollars

My soldier son
Returned from the bush
He brought back shattered hands
A burnt and livid face
That terrified his mother
But he brought back money
So we went to the city
Got these passports
And now we're here

Hereafter

Soleïman Adel Guémar

It's weird, but I wasn't even scared for a second when they came! I heard their hesitant steps on the dark corridor outside and I knew that this time, it was me they were coming for. They were walking quietly so as not to wake the others. I think it's mainly because of the rules that they do that. Whenever an inmate managed to shout out as they came to get him, they gagged him and dragged him down to the underground court at the double. I'd only just hear his last muffled screams, my ear pressed against the door, holding my breath.

I wasn't left waiting long – no more than three months, I think. I'd got used to my cell and the nauseating smells that came from the tiny hole I used for a toilet. There'd have been no point complaining. Nobody'd have listened. But in spite of everything, I was very lucky! Some ended up going totally crazy, waiting for long years on end for that fateful dawn. Me, I passed my time thinking of Samia and the sea. I was determined to be healthy in body and mind at the execution. After all, it was *my* execution, the only one I was ever going to have!

They were all very kind. The public prosecutor offered me a cigarette. I smoked it down to the filter. I knew I'd not be dragging on another for a while. Then the imam came to ask me to recite the chahada. He looked serious and fiddled nervously with a handsome set of green beads. As soon as he'd finished with me, two mastodons crashed me backwards against an upright girder set in the ground and tied me to it with a rope that smelled of burning. The soldiers in the platoon lifted their weapons – not very tidily – and fired! The mastodons fell, struck down. One bullet went through my thigh, another lodged in my stomach and a third did for my left eye. I was mad with joy. None had hit my heart. Not one. I was going to point this out to them, but some imbecile came and finished me off with a bullet in my neck. So I decided to keep quiet.

The next day, it was raining torrents when I saw the imam again, in the cemetery. He was wearing a black raincoat over his white gandoura. I recognised him straight away. My cousin Mourad was sticking close to him. I still owed Mourad money. I was glad to see that he'd come to my funeral. I knew it wouldn't be like him to begrudge me so little. He had shaved his moustache and was wearing my handsomest suit.

Practically all of them were there: Baba-Sliman's son-in-law Boualem, the country guard's son Kadour, Samia's father Si Larbi. Even Kaci-Tampouce, whose bicycle I'd stolen when we were kids, was there. I had tears in my right eye to see them weeping for me so sincerely and turning back every ten yards while walking away, at the risk of cricking their necks.

But what bad luck ultimately! I feel so sad I could die. Nobody talks here. They all act like they're dead and buried.

We Miracle-Workers

Zhila Irani

She was born into a religious family and grew up under the influence of a strict moral code. She aspired to the virtues of compassion, self-sacrifice and respect for others, but above all she valued knowledge and understanding. To be good was inseparable from being successful, and success was her route to happiness. She excelled at school and entered university.

Her student years coincided with the Iranian revolution and its aftermath. In that storm, several friends lost their lives and many more were arrested and detained. The revolutionary slogans about religious purity, freedom of speech, social justice and other lofty ideals were soon betrayed. The real intentions of the old clergy, the new politicians, quickly became clear.

The Shah's reign had brought relative freedom and equality for women. The new Islamic state undid those achievements, depriving women of all their rights. Women's sole role was to serve their menfolk. Some said that women must be banished from politics to counterbalance their immense power as mothers. The honour of being able to give birth, to become a mother, to make the family grow, constituted woman's essential character and her only official role. There were fewer and fewer opportunities for women to prove themselves. Inequality spread and deepened. But like other educated and thoughtful people, she rejected all this.

She wondered whether women's potential could be proved if only everything was painted black, so that women's capabilities could shine, like rays of light, through a sea of darkness. For only faith in the power of the pen, she feels, can bring about a new way of thinking – a new cultural revolution.

It is at this point that she puts pen to paper and works wonders.

Swansea Collage 2

Composed by Sylvie Hoffmann

*Based on conversations with asylum seekers, most of them from
French-speaking African countries*

Section 55: The friend's story

A young mother with baby
Stealing nappies.
The welfare state turns a blind eye.

Section 55: The daughter's story

I'm 18 years old.
I live on the buses
Just to keep going.

Section 55: The parents' story

Our eldest daughter taken away from us!
Kept behind in London, no money, no food, nowhere
To live, on her own, to be caught and sent back to be
Torn and abused by the military.
And yet they know! Themselves, the British, they're
Shitting themselves to get out of the embassy.
We want her with us
We want her safe
We want her well
We want to care for her
We are not given the freedom to love our own daughter.

Insomnia

Denounced – persecuted – exiled – dispersed –
Refused – sectioned – certified –
Now, how shall we proceed?

The M.P.'s surgery: interpretation

– What does she want me to write?
– Tell him I found no solicitor to take up my case.
Tell him where do I need to look?
Tell him I cannot pay for one myself.
Tell him I'm scared, my baby is babbling but I am scared.
– What does she want me to write?

The G.P.

This G.P., he won't examine me.
He examines my clothes instead,
He refuses to touch me.
He won't use Language Line.
He refuses to believe me.
He says I'm telling lies, he says I'm fine.
He gives me Prozac, a stronger dose each time.
It's destroying me, I cannot sleep.
They are the mad ones, not me.

Dispersal at work

My brother was sent to Swansea, he'd only just got here, he started to feel sick. Couldn't speak any English. One of his housemates called for an ambulance, took him to Singleton Hospital. Nurses told him to wait. Next thing, in came the police. The doctors must have called them. So they took him down to Swansea Central. They strip searched him. They kept him in a cell for ten hours, till three in the morning. He says to me: "I'm not staying in Swansea, I'm scared shit, I'm off."

He's fucked his NASS support!

Multiple occupancy

The arsehole, he brought a woman back.
I tried to sleep through the fights and screaming.
I couldn't, I fled into the night, I just ran,
That's why I'm here on your doorstep.

Anonymous statement

I was refused, evicted, left to starve. I went back to collect my mail from the new occupants. The woman, Middle Eastern, she speaks no English. I try to explain, I gesture, I mime the letter coming through the letterbox. I put my hand through the letterbox: she screams! She calls her husband. She's saying I want to come and move in! The husband's a big guy, big chest, big big threatening gestures! I'm only little – he's big and strong. But I want my letters!

He finally gets it, hands them over – only, all ripped up.

Madhouse

That morning I left for college
I didn't know I'd not be coming back.
I took no belongings, no books, no clothes – I did not know.
I'm lost here, utterly lost and bewildered.

Still in Swansea?

Yes, I'm still in Swansea. Even when you're destitute
You don't shit in the saucepan that you use to cook your food.

Roofless

– Where are you staying now?
– Oh, I haven't decided yet!
Prime ministers and presidents speak over my head.
Me, I want to stay in bed,
To sleep, sleep, since they won't let me work.
Sleep!
I want to sleep and die and yet I have to live.

Progress and True Progress

Maxson Sahr Kpakio

Dedicated to all Asylum Seekers and Refugees around the Globe: don't give up, but let the sky be your limit. There are still more good people than bad people in the world.

When I think of one kind act that I did today, or someone did to me today, however small, I know I am moving forward.

The power to change my life lies in my own mind. I choose to let go of self-defeating attitudes and replace them with positive thoughts.

Every moment, I am becoming more loving, more considerate, more generous, and more filled with positive thoughts.

I commit myself to the practice of quieting my mind and reflecting in silence, bringing myself closer to my soul and my highest potential.

There is nothing I cannot do if I put my mind to it.

The future awaits my dreams and the blueprint for success that I now create with my positive thoughts, even taking into consideration the very new environment that I find myself in.

Sometimes, because of people's attitudes towards me in this new environment, certain things try to hold me back; I then stumble, stop and re-think.

I measure my success by measuring how much I love, not how many things I acquire. I try my best to be kind and gentle in every situation. I try to disprove people's beliefs about me by telling them that I am not what they think or hear about me.

I no longer filter everything through anger, but let old resentments go and move into a brighter state of mind.

I improve the quality of my life with every positive thought. What I begin to practice now will become second nature. The dreams I envision are unfolding every moment.

Every forward step I have made in my life gives me confidence in myself. I take the time to appreciate how far I have come despite all the negative thoughts about me in my new home.

I know that I am moving forward because I don't sweat over the small stuff, and I am able to handle the big stuff with grace and dignity, even the acts of racism, hate, and prejudice.

I expand my perspective and my capacity for understanding every day, always taking the time to see good things in everyone. But do they do the same?

Each morning, I vow to approach everything with an open heart. I handle problems more easily than I did a month ago, a year ago, a decade ago, because I am committed to becoming the best person I can be.

I choose to envision only peace, harmony, and kindness. I take time to acknowledge the still, quiet place within me and draw strength, compassion, and wisdom from it.

I have abundant enthusiasm for life, in this part of the world that I am in today, and look forward to each new day.

Yesterday is just a vanishing thought. Today I have the opportunity to start fresh and create miracles. I realize that I am here for a brief moment, and I try to make the best of each day. Every day, I find a way to contribute something, no matter how small, to the goodness of the world, and particularly the community in which I live today.

I no longer force things to go my way, but instead, gently allow my inner knowledge to direct me. My old habit of controlling every second of my life is a thing of the past.

The stress I have accumulated in my life is fading away with each breath. During stressful times, I let go of the habit of complaining.

My new thinking allows me to laugh at myself when I stumble; to brush myself off, and to move forward with renewed energy.

There are no obstacles I cannot overcome with my inner resources, and I take the time to pause and reflect on the outstanding results I have achieved with my positive thoughts and inner wisdom.

I measure my progress by how calm and peaceful I remain when someone keeps me waiting, waiting, and waiting to hear about a final decision concerning my status in life; or when I lose something; or when someone abuses me for no reason, when someone keeps me waiting to be served, or when someone dashes my change, my cash, into my palm, as if my hands were too dirty to be touched.

Yes, I still try to measure my progress by how calm and peaceful I remain when someone looks in my face and tells me "go home where you come from", when someone betrays my interests and lets me down, when someone walks away from my life for no reason, or when I make a clumsy mistake. When any of these things occurs, I recall how I reacted to the same situation a year ago and congratulate myself on my progress, my true progress.

The Madness of Language

Anahita Alikhani

English is the most widely spoken language in the world, and is taught in every country. But spoken and colloquial English is very different from the polite language which is taught in schools. For somebody like myself, encountering the everyday language when we arrive in Britain can be very perplexing. For example, I've discovered that there is one word which can be used to express a huge range of feelings as varied as anger, disgust, happiness, joy, astonishment, drunkenness and so on.

An imaginary meeting between a foreign newcomer and a native of Britain can go something like this:

– Where are you from?

– Persia.

– Where the fucking hell is Persia?

– In Asia.

– Oh! Fucking long way from home!

– Oh yes!

– How's the weather there?

– Warm and nice.

– Oh! Fucking brilliant! What the fuck are you doing here?

– I'm a refugee.

– Oh, fucking asylum seekers! Pain in the arse!

– Excuse me, do you have a problem? Do you have piles?

– Fuck off!!!

– Excuse me, does this word mean yes or no?

– It means move your fucking arse and go to hell!

I can imagine that in a hundred years or so, as the language evolves, this word might be used even more widely, for example on the news: "This morning Her F'kin Majesty the F'kin Queen opened her f'kin Jubilee Celebrations . . ."

Swansea Babel Abertawe

By the "Writers in Exile" poetry group: Sylvie with Adel, Sally, Ruth, Ann, Walford, Aliou and Basil – writers from Algeria, England, France, Germany, Mali, USA and Wales

I seem to be German but really I'm not certain – am I European? –

If you tried hard & were a mythological blackbird, I would marry you, now that I am an opportunist –

I used to be someone's wife but now I ain't. I seem to be gentle & softly spoken but really I don't feel all right –

If you were a magician, I would be a red-golden Fabergé egg & I would behave differently, & myriads of drums would sound until I fell out of the sky –

I used to speak to myself, but now I'm careful: I don't want to be arrested. – But really, this is how it is! –

I used to steal but now I shout & scream & reach, with the audience, ecstatic heights –

If I were really free, I would dance on the sea-bed in the early dawn & if you were easier to live with, you would be my friend, until the oceans dry –

I used to be a bright-red pillar-box, but now I laugh at my folly –

If I were a cherry-blossom –

– Run out of time!

News from Iraq

Yosef Ali, Noser Sultani and Ahmed Zai
with Eric Charles

I

Noser Ali
Is a Baghdad spy
He sits on a seat by the Baghdad gate
To see when the Coalition comes
The Americans try to lure him
To tell them if he sees Saddam
He refuses the offer
Insisting:
I need a permanent job

II

Mr Ali
Speaks to the Iraqi people:
Brothers, sisters
American democracy
Is on the horizon

    Pause

Brothers and sisters wonder in silence
What's a horizon?
The sage shouts:
It's that line
Where the earth kisses the sky
It goes away
When you get closer

III – After the Fall

Mr Ali walks into his room
One hot afternoon
Sees his wife in bed
With another man
Runs to the kitchen
Fetches a knife
Suddenly stops
Shouts to his wife:

I'd kill you
Chuck your body to the birds
If I didn't belong to them

Thanking her fortune
She lifts her hands in the sky:
Allah saves us – and the Coalition!

IV – The Death of Noser Ali

The sage met his fate
At Baghdad gate
On his way to heaven
He goes to hell

Through the window he sees Saddam
Standing in shit to his neck
Looking at the angel he asks:
Why is Saddam in the shit to his neck
When Lenin has shit only up to his waist
The angel replies with a grin:
Lenin is standing on Stalin's head

The Text Committee

Abdalla Bashir-Khairi

The ball of talk is bounced between the three of them over and under the polished, shining surface of the glass table. Sometimes they swap languages. All around lie dossiers: fabricated trials, transcripts of interrogations of persons as yet unborn, denunciations of others who have been as good as dead for decades. This is the office and guardroom of the 'revolution' which they launched, suddenly, in order to accomplish what they call a 'most sacred task': to purify the whole realm of words of all that is not 'gentle and becoming'. It is an ideal office, set up in an ideal township, or so the official representative proclaimed in his inaugural speech.

Eyes roll in sockets, following the ball of talk, directing and possessing it. Today's session is a 'point of departure'. So, slyly skilful silence, manipulations of gestures, turns of heads, all of the subtleties of body language hope to conceal important secretive exchanges and thus to help the ball take short-cuts through a clandestine maze of expressive absence, while leaving it free of any apparent marks of conspiracy. And no wonder, for the three eminent men who are rolling this ball are all legends of craftiness. They are, as that inaugural speech put it more than a decade ago, 'the best of men for the best of weighty tasks'.

Cups of coffee and other refreshments surprise the receding shadow of noon, but still they sit, by their standards, straight, and solicit a place on the table for the new family of glasses now being carried in on silver trays, the gleam of which bewitches the beholders' minds. They are indeed in need of these digestifs, for the breakfast meal was rich and sumptuous, and a heated encounter is just behind them. Only a moment before, the maestro of the tribunal concluded his smart summing-up of the exchange so far. He assigned to himself, long ago, the task of writing the idealising reports refusing permission for any text that fails to restrict itself to the literal precepts of the official dispensation. In today's report, the maestro has outdone himself by utterly demolishing the three elements of time past, present and future. He has deconstructed the machine of time, bolt by bolt, and turned its wheel back to the days of superstition. Oh yes, a true maestro!

Their facial expressions relax with the passing of time and the receding shade. For they have completed the day's task to the utmost perfection. They are a tribunal of mighty ones, oh yes, true descendents of Sibawayh. So ingenious are they in correcting texts that not even a crow that traverses the township's heavens and cries out 'ka!' can escape the tight net of their grammar. Indeed, any such crow would be forced down to the ground and have his flying suit stripped off and torn to shreds; he'd even be shorn of a parachute, if wearing one. They'd tell him: "It's 'kaw', not 'ka'!"

To these oppressive adepts are due the poll-taxes of speech. Through them alone all texts must pass, and none may be corrected except by their committee.

They thunder that the writer of the play *The Cock of Al-Hajja Bahana* must spell the title differently. And they add, in an insinuating tone: "What do you *really* mean by the cock of Al-Hajja Bahana, anyway? And *who* do you mean, eh?!" Before he answers this question himself, the maestro says haughtily: "Leave the text here with us to correct the linguistic errors with which it is no less than rife. Go and don't come back until we summon you!" This is how the Tribunal Committee for Textual Rectification, known as the Text Committee for short, runs its affairs. And faced with ever increasing numbers of texts, it strains towards 'containing the phenomenon', in the impressive phrase of the brainy maestro, by further extending the reach of its effectively unlimited powers.

The playwrights, writing from living experience, have soon filled the Text Committee's files to overflowing with their scenes. But the fate of the poets is yet more grievous! The newspapers publish only sour and rotten little poems, miserable caterpillars of poems, scrunched up for fear of the tempest.

Some send their writings back to the homeland, from exile. But the Text Committee closes down any publishing houses that even give these writers the time of day. The maestro abhors them as 'lunatics'. He vehemently argues in a television interview that the 'character' who wrote the 'so-called' novel *The Wanderer* draws his ideas from the French Existentialists. "Where is *our* National Cultural Heritage in this audacious text of his? Damn him, the deranged heretic!"

As for the poet who published the two collections *The Rose at Evening* and *Why do the Emigrants not Return?* – the maestro says that his rhymes aren't metrical, that is, not symmetrical like a well-constructed building. And what's more, the maestro adds, his handwriting is very bad!

The next morning, in a frenzied 'sacramental ritual', the Committee burns all texts by members of the Literary Society, closes down that group's cultural centre, and appoints a new editorial board for the group's cultural magazine. The cultural centre is moved to a new site, out of sight (and out of mind), where they can enjoy torturing the magazine to death!

Short excerpts from texts by members of the group are broadcast on state television, accompanied by official warnings like those on packs of cigarettes, followed by the appearance of the Committee's members laughing while they toss, like adept grammarians, the ball of speech between themselves.

Note

A "Text Committee" or "Tribunal Committee for Textual Rectification" really is responsible for censorship in Sudan. It was once controlled by writers and artists, but since the military coups of 1985 and 1989 and the imposition of Islamic shariah law, the committee has been an instrument of cultural political oppression. Sibawayh "the Phonologist" was a great early scholar of the Arabic language (8th century AD). The popular drama The Cock of Al-Hajja Bahana, *by Adel Ibrahim, really did fall foul of the censors.* The Wanderer *is an unpublished novel by a friend of the author, and the other literary examples are invented. The "Literary Society" of the story is based on the Sudanese Society for the Humanities, which published the magazine* Horouf (Letters) *in 1988-9 until the regime closed them down. One of the author's articles, due to have been published in the magazine, was confiscated and used against him in his interrogation.*

TC

Two Poems

Mahmood Ahmadifard

Foreigner

This is Iran, the land of the Persians,
The land of Cyrus the Great,
The land of Darius and Xerxes.

An ancient people, a great people,
A familiar land, my country.

It is the land of the Sun, of the God of Love,
And thousands of years later
It is a land of cruelty and revolt.

The land of Gods is a despotic empire
Where workers are unpaid and bosses pillage – thieves!

Here even the trees are afflicted,
And the breeze, the spring, the harvest too, the rain.
Here the red roses of affection have perished, and
The Sun of Love is bereft of its warmth.

The nightingales no longer sing of freedom.
The little flower-messengers bring no more happy news.
Here the measure of ability and skill consists in
Absolute obedience and silence.
Here even whispering is forbidden!

This is Iran,
A foreign land, an unfamiliar land, strange, alien!

Unexplained

In this painless time
Of what pain should I complain?
Of what sorrow should I sing?
When pain and grief are stories not to be told,
When only grief rises from the innermost soul!

Lila

Hamira A. Geedy

"What if your arm's been broken, mum?" said Lila through her tears. "Please don't cry, sweetheart," her mother said, "I can put up with that man's cruelty, but I can't bear it when you get so upset." She tried to convince Lila that it was no big deal. It wasn't the first time her husband had shouted at her and beaten her, and it wouldn't be the last. Her children had often asked her to divorce him, but she always said she didn't want to lose them. "That's the law in this country. Only the father has the right to have the children." Lila knew there was just no point discussing it.

* * *

"What a pity!" Lila's friend Maria exclaimed. "I wish you could read this book too!" "But Maria, you know I can't. And you know why." Lila's father, Mr Ali, worked for the authorities. He was vain, ill-educated, superstitious, narrow-minded, and a traitor. He had betrayed his brother-in-law, who had been involved in the political struggle for Kurdish human rights. His brother-in-law had been arrested, tried and hanged by the authorities. Ever since then, Mr Ali's wife had suffered from depression. Lila knew he would never allow his children to go to school.

She asked Maria to read the book to her. Maria read: "Men and women were created equal. Both were run out of Paradise for the same mistake, both go to Hell for the same sins, so they should both have equal rights her on earth, in our society." Lila stared at her friend. "Can you teach me to read?" "Have you never tried to learn?" Maria asked. "Yes, once, I got an alphabet book, but my father threw it away. He said I should never read such trash, only the Koran. And he can't even read that! But I want to learn, I want to be able to help mum. Help her cope better and get out of the whole mess somehow." "Of course I'll teach you," said Maria. "You know, if your father could read the Koran, he'd probably not be so cruel to you all. The Koran says that a husband and father is responsible for his family, and it says that every human being is equal. That's what all the great religious books say, in fact. And Mohammed also said that from the day of our birth to the day of our death we should always try to study and learn."

* * *

Her mother was apprehensive. "How can you do such a dangerous thing? What if your father finds out?" "He mustn't, that's all. But I'm so happy. I love learning with Maria. I don't care what my father thinks. I want to learn and study so I can defy the tyranny of the authorities. As a great man once said: the only thing we have to fear is fear itself." "I understand, darling. But to be a woman in this society is a bad deal. It's for you that I put up with your father. Thank God my children are healthy and good."

* * *

It was a warm summer night. Her father was out. Lila sat by the window, looking at the sky. The stars shone like diamonds, and a young moon was rising, throwing his silver light on her beautiful face.

"Can't you sleep?" whispered her mother.

"I can't stop thinking," Lila said. "Ever since Maria taught me how to read and write, I've been wanting even more to go to school, to study, to go to university. I wish I was a boy, mum."

"What would you do then?"

"There are so many things. I could go out of the house! Men have so much more freedom. Men can be judges, women can't.

Men can divorce their wives, women can't divorce their husbands. Men can say no, women can't. The point is basically: men here have every right, women have no rights. Men despise women here."

"Not all of them. There are many families where the girls go to school, even to university. Many girls are studying medicine, engineering."

"Yes, but if that's so common, why can't women be judges?"

* * *

The next morning Lila's father came home and picked a quarrel with his wife. He barked in his coarse voice: "Where's Lila?" "She's visiting Maria," his wife replied in a low voice, looking at him with a strange gleam in her eyes. At that moment Lila came back, with a book in her hand. "Hello dad." She stood firmly. He stared at her, speechless at first, shaking with rage. The silence grew for a few moments, then he exploded. "You – you slut!" he shrieked at his wife, then he turned on Lila. "Where did you get that – thing?" "This is a book, dad. I got it from Maria's house," Lila replied quietly.

Mr Ali rushed into the kitchen to get something to beat her with, but happened to see a kettle full of boiling water.

* * *

Lila spent eight weeks in hospital. Police officers came and filled in their forms. They knew exactly what had happened but they did nothing about Mr Ali. It was their belief that a husband and father has the right to treat members of his family exactly as he chooses. At Lila's bedside, her mother protested, but the policemen replied: "Your husband tells us you don't pay deference to him. He is the head of the family. You owe him respect. That's what he told us to tell you."

* * *

"Thanks be to God, Lila, your face has no marks." "But all my body, my neck, my breasts, are scarred." "Don't worry, darling. You remember your aunt who lives in England. She promised to help you. She's sent money to buy a passport and go to stay with her. She says she'll even help you study."

* * *

They had the money, but neither Lila nor her mother could get a passport. The officials told them that Mr Ali would have to come and make the application on Lila's behalf.

"But he won't. And my daughter has to go to England. She needs medical treatment."

"We have excellent hospitals here in Iran."

"But for her to have an operation here, her father needs to sign to give permission. And he won't."

"Well, she should get married, then her husband can give his permission."

As they left the office, Lila's mother said out loud: "Thank God I can breathe, at least, without permission!"

* * *

The afternoon sun shone in upon the colourless, still face. Lila's heart wanted to stop at the thought of her mother dead. She had tried to buy a passport for Lila from a smuggler, but Mr Ali, like a cat, smelled everything. In his loud, brutish voice he yelled: "You think I'd let you send my daughter away to a foreign country?"

"I want to help her!" Lila's mother dared to raise her voice. "How could you be so cruel to burn her poor body!"

"That's it! I've had enough!" Mr Ali flipped. He took his wife's head and crashed it against the wall. He was very strong. Lila burst in and tried to pull him back but he pushed her away and carried on with the attack on his wife. Even when she was lifeless, he went on beating her.

51

When the officials saw the corpse, Mr Ali told them she had tripped on the stairs. There was no investigation. He warned the children not to say anything.

* * *

They forgot laughter. They lost all confidence. They were not even allowed to communicate with friends and neighbours.

Two years later, Lila's little brother Amir turned 18. Since he had no education, he joined the army. The goodbyes were very sad. Lila wept. "I think God must have forgotten us. How can I stay here without you, with this man?"

"Don't say that," Amir replied. "God has not forgotten us. I'm sure it'll be OK, somehow. We'll be free one day, I'm sure."

They hugged.

Meanwhile, on the stairs outside their room, Mr Ali was cleaning his rifle. Suddenly they heard the loud bark of gunshot. They froze. Then Amir rushed through the door to see their father lying in a pool of blood. He had accidentally killed himself. They didn't know whether to cry for grief or joy. Amir said: "I told you God had not forgotten us. The voice of that bullet was the voice of God."

* * *

After the funeral, Ali tried to stay to help her, but he had to go to the army. Lila was desperate to get a passport and go to her aunt in England. She needed a husband to give permission for her to travel. Her cousin agreed to marry her just for that purpose. So she was able to get to London.

But very soon her aunt's husband was telling her: "You have no right to go outside alone. And mind what you wear. Cover your arms. You have no right to speak to any man," and so on. They wanted her as a house servant. She felt she had no choice but to obey. Three months later she managed to leave their house and move somewhere else. But there was no way she could afford plastic surgery. She didn't know what she was supposed to do. She couldn't study either. She had no identity. Her aunt and her husband had taken her passport and torn it to pieces. She doesn't know what she's supposed to do. She has no identity. She has no right to claim benefits. She certainly cannot get a student grant. She has no right to work – she has no National Insurance number. She cannot claim asylum – she has been in this country too long already. From a poor country under a harsh dictatorship, she has come to a highly civilised, wealthy country with a well-developed infrastructure. Yet still she is desperate.

Lila is another victim of – what do you think? – her father's narrow-mindedness? Society? Culture? Governments? What do *you* think?

May 2004: Lila is still living in London, destitute and homeless, dependent on friends. All names have been changed.

Three Poems

Eric Ngalle Charles

An ancient Iroko tree

In the village square
Stands an Iroko tree
A meeting place for our mothers
They rest their backs and baskets after
A day's labour at the plantation
At times we run
Our protruded stomachs
Meeting them half-way
With sweaty and burdened wrinkles
They embrace us
Under that ancient tree
A cornerstone for village gossip
A meeting place for village chiefs
In its tall branches
Squirrels hide their fortunes
A branch falls
Every time a stranger walks by
On dark nights
The large eyes of an owl
Scan the environs
An ill omen
Faint in the distance
The village drum
The Njimbi is playing
Birth of a child
A boy

A girl
The gods are not to blame
Says the village medicine man
Old Iroko tree
On its feet
The village rests
Leafless tree
Telling tales
To a listener

A stranger's tale

My village name's Ngalle
"Eric!" my mother calls
When I am wrong
        I was born in Mboam Soppom
        A small town
        Along the meandering slopes
        Of Mount Cameroon
I am twenty-four
With a daughter
And a step-daughter
I have been married twice

The first unofficial
Her name Natalia
From Sochi
The Russia Riviera
By the mountain of Ahun
The second
Deborah
This was official
From Ely
Not so hard to find from here
One morning after a family feud
I lent my hands to a stranger
He called my name
I opened my arms
Blinded by the need to escape
He showed me the continents
From the heat of Mboam Soppom
To the cold terrain of Russia
Till I landed in Wales
When I was a Zimbabwean
The good deeds of my encounters
I tell
But the nightmares
Will forever be mine

My alien self

For my daughter Jolie

I left my prison cell
My trapped mind
      In my endless search I strayed
Finding freedom in a new abode
Leaving behind
My alien self
      But when can I return to my utopia
      Strangers wait
      With poisoned eyes
      Hunters lay traps
      On the waysides
Let my flag of poetry sail
Filling the vacuum
That housed my mind
For the love of my child
I shall empty the cavities of my breast
      So the land be blessed
Jolie, since you came
I'll never return again
To my alien self

This, or the Deluge...!

Abdalla Bashir-Khairi

Suddenly that evening, as I was beginning to turn my steps towards the far corner of the vast square at the centre of the city, I felt a constriction in my chest and an unusual commotion. Before I could complete my quick turn to face the other side of the square, I found myself in their hands.

The sun was bidding farewell to the quarters of the square; dusk was dragging the sun's golden tails in a slow and leisurely retreat towards its hidden sleeping-place, behind the distant horizon, beyond the Nile. I could no longer see the radiant faces and white robes of those who had committed themselves to beautifying the city streets with the roses and flowers of the New Thinking. I bade the city and them farewell in my thoughts and feelings. Since then I have seen neither it nor them. It was as if celestial carriages drawn by winged horses had transported them all, that evening, to invisible heavens – or so I consoled myself.

They severed the thread of my contemplation and bundled me into a Landrover, then deliberately confused my senses by taking a long, roundabout and zigzag route. At one moment we seemed to be passing over a river. I felt a whiff of a soothing draught of air waft over me, refreshing hope within me, despite the tight blindfold. The car stopped several times. Various exchanges took place between those inside it and others, all in the form of codes and riddles.

Finally we stopped at what seemed to be the destination. I was dragged along a long, damp hallway, half-walking, almost suffocating, roughly shoved, stumbling, until at last I arrived in a kind of circular room at the end of the hallway. There I was stripped of all of my clothes, cruelly beaten, flesh and bone, and I suffered – momentarily – humiliation. This was followed by hours of interrogation inside that damp room smelling of betrayal.

The face interrogating me was so sadistic that it seemed visibly to thrive on the sight of me twisting and convulsing under the whips of pain. It was as if that character had sprouted like a fungus from spores of professional crime and vileness. Or it seemed as though he was extracting from my flesh and my soul the price of an old vendetta, or exacting revenge for blood that had been shed unknown to me. It was a face absolutely isolated from any current of mercy and all that belongs with it: a maliciously ugly face, oozing with insult and the will to injure everything innocent.

They want to wrest a confession out of me? A confession of what? Of a conspiracy which they suspect? He handed me an exercise book and a pen, and with a glare which gathered all the menace of the world, in a coarse voice, home to all of cruelty's parasites, he said: "I want this back tomorrow morning, full of the names of all who were with you and with all the details of the conspiracy! No need for you to deny your knowledge of anything, our sources have left us in no doubt." He gave me a meaningful look as he shut the door behind himself: "Do what we ask of you, and we'll make you a prosecuting witness."

Rage possessed me and I shouted at him: "Some of us have met their Maker under your filthy hands, but those who still have that to come still do as they please under the sun and under the moon. Didn't you arrest us from a square at the heart of the city?"

My voice was lost to the wind and air: already he had locked the door behind him, slipping out without hearing me. I picked up the exercise book which he had left. But the pen had fallen and rolled away. I crawled towards it, exhausted to the extreme. My fingers groped their way towards it over the damp floor. When I was satisfied that my hand held the pen, as far as my worn-out strength permitted I straightened up, hugged the exercise book and pen to me and breathed the sweet repose of the enchanted passion of two intimate companions in an oasis in a desert of nothingness. I put the exercise book down on the ground and bent over it to write. My eyes were now used to the semi-darkness hovering over that place. Of which enough.

As I was immersed in writing, the door was half-opened. I didn't raise my face, but I heard him say: "We were sure you'd act like a rational, intelligent man." He closed the door behind him and disappeared, adding: "Keep on writing, and don't forget you'll be a key witness."

The sound of the door closing synchronised with a strange relaxation in my exhausted memory. I remembered how, when I was being beaten and kicked, I had rolled myself up and completely surrendered to the experience moment by moment. Exactly in that position I relived, in an enlightened and vivid way, the events of our historic procession, the White Procession which reclaimed the long road from Al-Mahdiyya to Sharfi Graveyard. I had been lucidly alive with the White Procession as it turned, following the road to the left to head past the Northern Police Station, and on towards Martyrs' Square at the heart of the city. The men were wearing white jallabiyyas and bright turbans, and the women were wearing white dresses. The procession was radiant, peaceful and wonderful. I particularly recollected how all of us, men and women, white-haired elderly and children, sat on the ground, when obstructed by the police, in a composed, reverent and sober manner, each person in his own place.

I rolled myself up more in an attempt to protect my sensitive organs from the humiliating, damaging kicking. The remembrance continued, alive and vivid. People gathered around us and on the rooftops of the houses, women and men astonished at our bright whiteness seeping down towards the

60

square. So we poured on, a silent flow, from the left of Mahatma Gandhi Junction, into Nile Street, and under the eves of the Sudan Broadcasting Corporation building, where we were grievously shocked to see *them* giving a very old man an excruciating beating. From there the procession headed through Khalifa's Square, to the court where the judges sat in a row, empty-hearted, holding their noses high, haughtily strangling themselves with their neck-ties, like some satanic beings which have emerged from a dark cosmic hole.

I cannot now remember anything further than that, and I no longer have the strength to continue this narration, for the mere act of evoking memories wears me out, and the remains of the candle's glimpses inside myself drip and fuse into a formless whole before, finally, being extinguished!

It doesn't matter. I am, inevitably, dying now. In just a few moments I will be irrevocably deceased, and my soul will have what is arguably the good fortune to observe the last stages of the hidden crime in my poor visible body lying on the ground, motionless.

Of course, my oppressor will be back for the exercise book, expecting to break the pen after forcing me to sign my name. But when he sees me a lifeless corpse, he'll be struck dumb, and his disappointment will rise as he understands that the exercise book is only an empty pad of pages eying him sarcastically. . . .

Note

"This, or the Deluge....!" describes the "White Procession" in Khartoum in 1985, a peaceful protest organised by the non-violent democratic movement known as the Republican Brothers (the members and leadership included many women). The Republican Brothers were inspired by "Africa's Ghandi", Al-Ustaz Mahmoud Taha, whose arrest, trial and execution for 'apostasy' in 1985 was triggered by his pamphlet "Hatha Aow Al-Tawafan" – "This, or the Deluge". See www.alfikra.org

TC

Africa, Mother

Aliou Keita

Africa, mother, I am thinking of you
Black African woman, thank you
Mother who carried your son on your back in the night
When everyone was sleeping
To console him
Woman of the family work in big fields, forests and bushes
Mother who searched for dry wood to cook a meal
When everyone was hungry
To feed us
I am thinking of you
Tireless black woman of Maniga Big Family

Africa, my Africa, I am thinking of you

It is time to get together
To decide to work and to eat together
To ban war and tribal fighting together

In the early morning I take my bag and walk
I know I'll see birds and hear them cry and sing
Announcing the coming of the rainy season

I'll see snakes crossing the road on my way to the farm

Peanuts, milk potatoes and yams will be plentiful after
                                          the rainy season

I will unite the people and bring the produce to them
To feed up my mother Africa

Proud warriors in the ancestral savannah

Africa, my Africa, I am thinking of you
Africa, mother
Thank you for everything you have done for me

Eight Poems

Soleïman Adel Guémar

Homage

at last I'll be able to love you until the dawn
erase from your eyes the languid depthless nights
spent waiting for me at the bedside of our dreams
while on the damp earth of a prison cell somewhere
in the world of men spiders played with my hair

Fire of joy

land bled dry
murdered unceasingly
will you ever give birth
to the child I'm expecting of you

The keywords

I don't know the words
that open wide the doors
you have to go through
folded doubly in two

Illusions

and we thought we were back together again
in a land of asylum
while others
hiding in the
border shadows
were already waxing their
nearly new boots
but you didn't know it yet

you dreamed of a city where birds
make their nests by every window
you dreamed while others
were already marching
eager to trample over
the flowers in your garden
watered with your blood
but you didn't know it yet

you were getting ready to join
the jubilant crowd
while whole columns
of others
were smashing their way
in through the city gates

and when you thought you heard
their nearly new boots
resounding
on the smoking tarmac
it was already too late

Known places

on the wall
blood drying

the child disarticulated
lies beside her mother
– long black hair pretty –
half calcified
in her flowery dress

on the road
remains of bodies
swollen by heat
eaten by animals

in the looks of those escaped
certain shadows
sail

the burned field
still smoking

here monsters passed

Interrogatory

back to the wall
I watch my life
pass by and my eyes
are black holes where
light disappears

this inhuman stink rises
it contaminates my torturers
and the whole world
each time I fall
head first
from the top of the metal ladder
my groans are silent

my body
inert
still recalls the scent of flowers
and gorgeous sunsets

I want to die like this
to die on them
ultimate escape
assault on the troops' morale
to be buried beneath X
or in a common ditch
to be able to dream at last
in peace

A dream

the storks have come back
to make their nests on the highest
rooftops the wind is rising
over the blue lake
rocking the motorboat and the orphan
is signaling to you from the shore
through the swirl of dead leaves
the naked trees
are stretching their arms up into the sky
which is watching you smiling at last

Exile

1

my country
gives off a scent
which calls you by your first name
the moment you turn your back

your heart squeezes
as at your first embrace

2

having come back from so far
if you ever
can't find the way here to us
stop
and contemplate the mountains
you think you know

ask passers-by
why the fountain's dry
where these paths go
that drop into exhausted commas

if ever
you come back from as far
as my daring takes me
we'll walk together
one day maybe
beside precipices

3

my lunar memory
has woven flying carpets

The Wanderer

Anonymous, Anglo-Saxon, about 1200 years old
Translation: Steve Short

"Often the outcast abides in grace,
The Maker's mercy, though troubled in mind
He has had to stir the ice-cold sea
For long with his hands, to embark on exile's path
Throughout the ocean: fate is fully fixed."

So said the wanderer, awake to hardships,
Fierce struggles and the slaughter of kinsmen:

"Often each morning I have had alone
To lament my anguish. There is no-one alive
That I dare openly express
My thoughts to now . . .

. . . He who tries it knows
How cruel a companion sorrow is
To he who has few beloved friends:
Not twisted gold but the path of exile absorbs him,
Not the world's fame but the frozen heart . . .

. . . Often when sorrow and sleep together
Hold fast the abject exile, it seems
To him in his mind that he embraces
And kisses his lord, laying on his knee
His hands and head, as he heretofore
Received gifts from the throne in the days of old:
Then the friendless man wakes up again,
Seeing before him the fallow waves,
The bathing sea-birds speading their feathers,
Falling snow and ice immingled with hail.

Then are the heart's wounds heavier,
Sore about loved ones. Sorrow is renewed
When the imagination visits memories of kinsmen,
Greeting them gladly, examining each part eagerly.
But a man's associates swim away again,
The floating minds do not bring many
Familiar spoken words there. Care is renewed
In him who must send his worn-out heart
Frequently over the frozen waves.
Therefore I cannot think why throughout
This world my mind does not grow dark . . .

. . . Truly a man may not be wise before he owns
A deal of winters in the world . . .

. . . A clear-sighted man must know how shocking
It will be when the wealth of this world stands waste,
As now in various places throughout this middle-earth
Walls stand wind-blown,
The snow-swept ramparts rime-covered,
The wine-halls crumble, their owners lie
Stripped of revelry, their valiant retinues
All dead, fallen by the wall. Some war carried off,
Snatching them away; one a bird took
Over the deep sea; one the grey wolf
Dealt his death; one lord a tear-stained man
Hid in a grave beneath the earth.
So man's Maker demolished this city
Until, robbed of the revelry of the citizens,
The ancient work of giants stood deserted."

Then he who has wisely considered this creation,
And deeply contemplated this dark life,
Will, wise at heart, often call to mind
Many past struggles, and speak these words:

"Where has the horse gone? Where has the hero gone?
　　　　　　　Where has the treasure-giver gone?
Where have the benches for banquets gone? Where is the
　　　　　　　bliss of the hall?
Alas the bright goblet! Alas the mailed warrior!
Alas the prince's majesty! Truly that time is past,
Darkened beneath the helm of night, as if it never were!
Now there stands in the track of that dear troop
A stupendous wall, painted with serpent-shapes.
Many ash-spears have slain those warriors.
Weapons greedy for carrion, an unconquerable fate,
And storms batter these stony slopes.
Snow falling in showers shackles the earth
In winter's grip. The gloom comes,
Night's shadow grows dark, and sends from the north
Fierce driving hail on men in malice.
Ordered fate makes worse the world under heaven.
Here wealth is fleeting, here a friend is fleeting,
Here man is fleeting, here kin are fleeting.
All the foundations of earth will be deserted."

So the wise man said to himself, sitting apart in thought.

Worthy is he who holds to his faith. A man must never
　　　　　　　make known too easily
The bitterness in his heart, unless he knows how
　　　　　　　to heal it beforehand –
That warrior who can accomplish it with courage.
　　　　　　　It will be well with him who seeks grace,
Comfort from the Father in heaven, where a haven
　　　　　　　waits for us all.

Two Poems

Aimé Kongolo

The grief of war – Le chagrin de la guerre

Pagaille, confusion et impudique guerre mauvaise.
Ô, guerre mauvaise!

Shambles, confusion and shameless, vile war.
O, vile war!
Where is my father?
O, family of vipers!
Where are the innocents?
You took them with no pledges.

Why are you so senseless?
You who plant them, the innocents, in a garden of death –
Why did you make me so wretched?
You've taken them on an eternal journey
Without looking back
Knowing that each child's life is a search for the father.

When will your raging hunger be satisfied?
Even the new-borns, you come and take them constantly.
Accursed be you who call us to that feast –
You killer of innocents.

O war, where have you taken them?
You have left me only grief.
Where did you lead them?
Bring them back once more onto this long path,
Onto the human road along which we carry our sufferings,
Our tiredness and our hunger each without end.

Woe to the warriors who ruin our fates.
Despite the bombardments, the earthquake,
We walked after we had suffered.
Bring them onto this unsure road where we suffer
                                                    unwillingly
And where there is jealousy, envy, hatred and despair,
Despair which makes us unable to live, unable.

You who inhibit the innocents in living –
You who inhibit them as they walk on this unsure road –
On this path through a pitiless universe of brutal conflict –
Stabs in the back too common, innocent passers-by too
                                                    easy prey,
And all one breathes and all one sees is only pain, grief
And blood upon human blood.

Et tout ce qu'on respire et qu'on voit n'est que douleur, chagrin
Et les sangs humains.

Les réveils de l'Amour

Lève-toi! lève-toi!
Lève-toi, ma chérie
Lève-toi, mon amour
Car j'ai besoin de regarder
Les yeux qui brillent comme
Le soleil brille sur la mer
J'ai besoin d'entendre ta voix douce
J'ai besoin de voir ton visage
Qui brille des joies de l'amour
Des joies de l'amitié
Des joies de l'affection
Profonde de notre amour
Je t'aime! Je t'aime!
Je t'aime comme mon jardin
De l'enfance
Je t'aime comme le jardin
D'hiver
Je t'aime comme le jeudi Saint
Je t'aime comme le jour de l'An
Je t'aime! Je t'aime!
Car ton nom commence par

A

A comme la première lettre de l'alphabet
A comme le verbe avoir
A comme aimer, A de l'amour
A de l'amitié,
A de l'affection intense
A comme Alice au Pays des Merveilles
Lève-toi! ma chérie
Lève-toi! mon amour

Love's Awakening

Wake up! Get up!
Wake up my darling
Wake up my love
I need to look in
The eyes that shine as
The sun shines on the sea
I need to hear your gentle voice
I need to see your face
That shines with the joys of love
The joys of friendship
The joys of affection
The deep affection of our love
I love you! I love you!
I love you like the garden
Of my childhood
I love you like the garden
Of winter
I love you like Good Thursday
I love you like New Year's Day
I love you! I love you!
For your name begins with
A
A like the first letter of the alphabet
A like the verb avoir to have
A like aimer to love, A for amour
A for amitié friendship
A for affection intense
A like Alice in Wonderland
Wake up! my darling
Wake up! my love

The Poet's Garden

Soleïman Adel Guémar

In a country where business fever was spreading at the speed of sound, carried by the mysterious world-wide "hafmorstuff" virus, lived a poet who still believed in beauty and the sublime values of the simple life. He had chosen to isolate himself on the roof-terrace of a high-rise apartment block, where he lived in an old washroom, three metres by two, happily contemplating the splendid sunrises and sunsets visible from his perch above the city.

Happily, until one day an uncommon idea entered his head: to convert this aerial-infested, otherwise uninhabited space into a pretty little garden. But this was impossible, as he was well aware. He brushed the ludicrous idea away. But at that moment he must have been unconscious of the power of his utopia. For he was unable to rid his mind of the image of a garden as lovely as those of ancient Babylon, hanging over a city which once had been beautiful, now made unbearably ugly by its inhabitants.

And so he came to know the agonies of insomnia and the terrible lassitude of days and nights without end. "If I could only get hold of a plot of land far from the city! That would be so much easier!" he thought to himself. And in an excess of optimism he went to consult the city council.

He knocked on several doors which remained closed, indeed double locked, and was obliged to spend several entire days waiting in icy corridors, so that he caught a bad cold, but everywhere he got the same response: Lots of money! Dozens and dozens of millions! And what's more: at least ten years waiting time.

Blowing his nose quietly so as not to disturb the other people waiting at the bus station, he ruminated on his dreams and frustrations. An hour later he felt the crowd carry him to the back of a bus. His dreams jumped off and his frustrations, stronger than ever, tugged at his baggy clothes and his sagging skin, making him look quite pitiful. All around, squashed bodies talked and talked. And a moment later he saw them turn into a flock of sheep and goats, bleating away.

"Baaa!" said the pretty goat opposite. "Baaa! Baaa!" replied her friend. He felt an insane urge to bleat as well. He went: "Baaa!" The crowd fell silent. Some stared. The gentle little poet burst out laughing.

That night he decided not to bother with permission from the city council, since they seemed to be allergic to any idea which didn't come from their own collection of thinking heads.

Over the following days, the residents of his part of town noticed that their neighbour was unusually agitated. The more reserved called him bizarre; others, as always, called him mad. He was busily filling big bags with soil which he poured onto the terrace. There was a week of coming and going. Then he bought seeds and set about sowing them in a geometrical pattern with a symbolic meaning known only to him. Nobody cared what he was up to with all this soil. "A poet's whim!" said some.

Years went by. People ambled in the streets. Housewives scrutinised shop windows and kids played cops and robbers. They'd all forgotten the poet's very existence.

Then came the day when Sidi-El-Hadj El-Thawri raised his head higher than usual in thanking god for having blessed him with a broad-shouldered son-in-law. His youngest daughter had just married an army colonel three times her age, already married and with seven children, having picked him up at an eventful evening do. "A daughter worthy of her father!" he was thinking complacently when he froze, not daring to believe his eyes. But by the time he'd rubbed them he knew that there really was a garden suspended high over the building. Recovering from his stupor, he ran for the nearest police station to notify the authorities.

"A garden! A dreadful garden! May I go blind, Inshallah, if I tell a lie!" cried Sidi-El-Hadj. At first the officer sitting behind his huge desk thought he was facing a madman. But at length he agreed to send a patrol to investigate the matter.

Disappointed by this lack of urgency, Sidi-El-Hadj decided to take matters into his own hands. "No need to bother my son-in-law over such a little thing! We can mete out justice ourselves!" And he went to inform the neighbourhood committee – of which he was the dominant member.

An immense crowd gathered to stare at the strange sight. Gigantic flowers reached out from the roof-terrace to hang over the void. Not just flowers but shrubs and enormous green plants. No one could ignore it. Something had to be done!

People's eyes were filled with something like horror – and perplexity. In worried tones they whispered to one another about the weird man living up there like a savage. "A garden on top of a block of flats! A scandal!" "A roof terrace isn't for growing flowers! It's for television aerials, or maybe for playing football or a bit of jogging. But a garden!" "Utter madness! Exhibitionism!"

All present felt a growing sense of imminent danger and of deepening unity in their shared hostility to the poet, and they devised ever more insulting terms for him.

"A garden! Where?" cried a sophisticated lady who was driving by in a luxury car. "That's all we need! A garden hanging over our heads!" She promised to speak to her husband, who had an important job in the civil service. "My husband will take steps!"

Meanwhile someone had been cleaning her superb car's windscreen with a piece of rag, and when she drove off at high speed, she flung the windscreen cleaner into the ditch without even noticing him. The rag landed on his battered face. There was no pulse. He was dead. That did it! Sidi-El-Hadj solemnly proclaimed: "May his soul be with God. He died working, he'll go to Paradise." "This is all that poet's fault!" cried a man with a massive paunch. "It is!" shouted the crowd. "Send the young boys home, there's gonna be a ruckus!" shouted the fat-belly, but the young boys wouldn't go.

"Let's all go up there and get him," ordered Sidi-El-Hadj.

The little poet had heard the noise of the crowd but had assumed that it was just another of those rows which had grown so common since the spread of hafmorstuff. However, when the noise continued he decided to take a look. Seeing a multitude of faces looking up, he turned his head by reflex and looked above him. But there was nothing to see but the radiant blue spring morning sky.

"Kill him! Kill him!" roared thousands of voices. The sight of him enflamed their ferocity and they raced for the entrance to the building. The poet recoiled in fear. Meanwhile Sidi-El-Hadj, propelled by the crowd, slipped on an orange peel and fell, hitting his head on the pavement such that his soul instantly departed from his body, fleeing at the rate of several light-years in a few seconds, only to end up squashed into a gigantic black hole. That really did it now! The sons and all those of the tribe of Sidi-El-Hadj chanted "Death! Death!"

Now there were rewards. Si-Mokhtar, the richest shopkeeper in the neighbourhood, promised five million. Still richer, Ammi-Madani, a notorious businessman, offered ten to whoever reached the terrace first and threw the poet off it.

Men were fighting one another to get up there. Each wanted to achieve this patriotic honour. There were two more dead, three seriously injured by being trampled, and two disappeared, according to the boys who had scaled the nearby trees in order to survey the situation. Further deaths and injuries occured as the mob ascended the stairways, but most of them lived to swarm out onto the roof-terrace.

The little poet was sitting at the foot of a willow tree, his back to the crowd, looking straight ahead. For a moment all were silent, following his look. But there was nothing to be seen – just the line of a horizon that remained quite distant. There was a heavy silence, until it was disturbed by a fat fly which had just stung the bleeding head of one of the wounded.

"Kill!" shouted a son of Sidi-El-Hadj, and they all fell on the poet, grabbed a part of him, and hurled him into the void.

The poet fell, fell. Some thought he was taking too much time over it. Others used the word miracle. Some leaned over to get a better view, only to fall themselves and be instantly splattered. And still the poet fell.

The garden was sublime. There were flowers of every colour and every possible shape. Nothing like them had ever been seen. One by one, the poet's attackers turned away from the spectacle of his fall to admire the splendours of his garden. Lovers opportunistically picked roses, while the elders dug up shrubs.

Alerted belatedly, the minister of the interior arrived, panting, with his fifty-strong bodyguard. "We'll see – don't touch anything! We'll see what we'll do about this garden! Trust me!" His arrival had shut the crowd up, and now they spent a quarter of an hour acclaiming him. He seemed put out that he hadn't had time to prepare a speech.

"First of all, we'll give this garden a name," he improvised. "From now on it shall be known as the Sidi-El-Hadj garden, in memory of that saintly man." There was another quarter of an hour of acclamation. "And now, everybody go home quietly!" barked a plain-clothes policeman brandishing a gun.

The days following the incident were absolutely calm. The men went about their daily occupations with a sense of having done their duty, with light hearts and heads held high. The housewives gathered outside chic shop windows and talked and talked. And the young boys played at being the little poet.

Dream 2

S. and H. D. Albertson

This is a letter of support written by Mr and Mrs Albertson of Portmead, on behalf of a Turkish-Kurdish asylum seeker. Only the names and the address have been changed.
Such letters can often tip the balance of judicial decisions.

196, Heol Robert
Swansea
3.4.04

It is with pleasure I write this reference for Adan. Adan has lived amongst us for fourteen months. We were all very apprehensive when we knew that an Asylum Seeker was coming to live among us, but we had no need to worry, she has been a joy to live next door to. She is kind caring and a wonderful mother to her two lovely children. They have blended in well with the community. Adan goes to school quite a few times during the week to learn English as she wants to work within the caring profession. She is already helping other Asylum Seekers to settle in and has made a lot of friends, her English is vastly improving and this benefits others who cannot speak English so well. Adan's children have also made a lot of friends in the neighbourhood and it is a pleasure to see them mixing so well with the other children.

We all hope Adan and the children can stay and hope this letter will help her to realize her dream of staying and belonging.

Yours faithfully
S. Albertson
H. D. Albertson

I'm a man!

Well, nobody's perfect.

Some Like It Hot (1959) © MGM

To know more about Hafan Books, go to **www.hafan.org** or
email **hafanbooks@yahoo.co.uk** or write to us:

c/o Heyokah Centre
2 Humphrey Street
Swansea
SA1 6BG

@caDemI

hybu llên • literature promotion

Cardiff International Poetry Competition 2005

First Prize £5000

Judges:
Les Murray
Gwyneth Lewis

With a total prize fund of £7000,
the Cardiff International is one of the biggest
poetry competitions in the UK

It is open to established poets and beginners alike –
all entries are anonymously judged

Winning poems will be published in
New Welsh Review and on the Academi website

Closing date: 28th January 2005

Poems must be unpublished, in English,
and no longer than 50 lines

Entry forms and further information available from:

Academi
PO Box 438
Cardiff
CF10 5YA

www.academi.org

exiled ink

An innovative magazine reflecting exciting, different voices in a new cultural environment

Literature Discussion Commentary

Published by **Exiled Writers Ink!**

– for free expression by exiled and refugee writers

– ensuring their voices are heard

www.exiledwriters.co.uk

Contact: Jennifer Langer

jennifer@exiledwriters.fsnet.co.uk

THE BODY SHOP ®

DEFEND HUMAN RIGHTS

The Body Shop believes that it is the responsibility of every individual to actively support those whose human rights are denied to them.

We support Amnesty International and we opposed the asylum seeker voucher scheme in the UK.

For more details visit:
www.uk.thebodyshop.com > **our values**

The Body Shop
The Quadrant
7 St Mary's Arcade
Swansea, SA1 3QW
01792 456318

New Fiction, Poetry & Drama from Wales

Parthian is an independent publisher. We're always interested in new voices, perspectives and stories. Many of our prize-winning new writers are contributing to a vibrant world of books, stories and opinions in Wales and beyond.

In 2004, look out for *Urban Welsh*, an anthology of short stories, and *Sideways Glances*, a look at five off-centre Welsh artists.

For information about our publications and/or for submission guidelines, please visit **www.parthianbooks.co.uk** or call **01239 612059** or write to us at:

> The Old Surgery
> Napier Street
> Aberteifi / Cardigan
> SA43 1ED

"Parthian has a well-deserved reputation as the most vigorous publishing house in Wales, bringing old and new writers to their readers" *Planet*

THE MEDICAL FOUNDATION
Caring for Victims of Torture

South West Wales Support Group

Keith Bowen (Chairman) 01792 391475
Margaret Marriott (Secretary) 01792 232224

Each year the Medical Foundation treats about 5000 clients, including children. Paid and voluntary staff provide medical and social care, practical assistance, and psychological and physical therapy. Regional support groups raise funds and awareness. New members are always welcome.

www.torturecare.org.uk

Registered charity no. 1000340

amnesty international
WORKING TO PROTECT HUMAN RIGHTS WORLDWIDE

swanseagroup

www.amnestyswansea.org

Contact Scott Westron, Joint Secretary,

on **07967 509590**

or **info@amnestyswansea.org.uk**

British Red Cross
Caring for people in crisis

The British Red Cross is part of the International Red Cross and Red Crescent Movement.

We help people and communities cope with crisis, both by responding to emergencies and by helping people to be better prepared to deal with crisis themselves.

For further information on services and volunteering opportunities please contact

Susan Roberts,
Senior Services Manager (Swansea)

01792 450050

ssroberts@redcross.org.uk

www.redcross.org.uk

Refugee Media Group in Wales

We work with editors & journalists to help ensure that the media reporting of asylum is factual & balanced. • The key to the project's success is the participation of the **Refugee Link Group**: men & women with direct experience of asylum, who are being trained & supported to work with the media, challenge negative myths & stereotypes, & promote positive & in-depth coverage. • By raising awareness of asylum & associated issues through refugees' & asylum seekers' own voices, we aim to ensure that men's & women's different stories & experiences are understood. • **The ultimate aim is to change public perception of asylum seekers, so as to improve community relations & encourage integration & inclusion.**

Members include the **Welsh Refugee Council**, Displaced People in Action, **Amnesty International**, Cardiff Council, **Welsh Local Authorities Consortium for Refugees & Asylum Seekers**, Cardiff University, **Oxfam** & SOVA (Supporting Others through Voluntary Action).

"I feel like nobody here, ashamed, like everybody hates me, but they don't know me – only they know what they read in the newspapers – & that's not me" – **M, Swansea** • "People are being beat up & killed sometimes just because they are asylum seekers – we didn't come here for this, we try to leave behind this, we try to find peace here but it's not possible, not with this media" – **A, Cardiff** • "How can people accept me when all they read is such rubbish? I don't blame them for fear of me, they believe what they read. I want to meet them & speak to them & tell them it's not true. No reason to have fear of me" – **Z, Swansea**

For more information please contact
Vanessa Bucolli
029 20874681 / 07951 785935
bucolliv@cf.ac.uk

Drop-ins
Swansea World Stars FC
Festivities
Practical support
Emotional support
Lobbying

Details at
www.hafan.org

"Refugees are Welcome Here"

"Newcomers and Locals United"

"Nobody's Perfect"

SOVA: Supporting Others through Voluntary Action

www.sova.org.uk

Plethu Project

The Plethu project is unique in terms of services to refugees and asylum seekers. Trained volunteer mentors provide a combination of emotional and practical support on a one-to-one basis to displaced people with a variety of issues. This support is vital in promoting acculturation and psychological well-being. The Plethu project also recruits and trains volunteers from the refugee and asylum seeking communities to provide peer support. **Funded by The Diana, Princess of Wales Memorial Fund and The Welsh Assembly.**

YANA Project

A drop-in centre providing social support, peer mentoring and befriending for unaccompanied refugee minors.

For more information please contact:

Anne Hubbard and Mike Murray

Tel: 02920 495281

Email: plethu@btconnect.com

Registered charity no. 1073877

dpia DISPLACED PEOPLE *in* ACTION
Pobl Di-le yn Gweithredu

The objectives of DPIA are:

- The relief of people who are displaced due to hostilities, persecution, oppression, discrimination, natural disasters or other like causes, and their families and dependants suffering need, hardship and distress.
- The advancement of their education.
- The provision of facilities for recreation and leisure-time occupations in the interests of social welfare and in order to improve their conditions of life.

DPIA involves asylum seekers and refugees in their new communities, on a voluntary basis, giving them meaningful and interesting uses of their time. We assess their existing skills and enable them to learn new ones, offering opportunities for training, activities, educational visits, and special projects, working in partnership with other voluntary organisations. We include asylum seekers and refugees in decision-making regarding project design, implementation and evaluation. DPIA has received project funding from The Diana, Princess of Wales Memorial Fund and The Community Fund. We welcome enquiries from potential donors, volunteers and trustees.

Contact: Richard Yeo
DPIA
CSV House
Williams Way
Cardiff
CF10 5DY

(029) 2041 5706

richarddpia_uk@yahoo.co.uk

Registered charity no. 1082176